Joe the Monkey and Friends

Learn About Spending Smart

A Big Giant Tale of Stuff

by John Lanza
pictures by John Lanza and Patrick Rooney

Snigglezoo media

Edited by Marilyn "Meerkat" Walton. I can't thank Marilyn enough for how much better she has made this entire trilogy of books. She has been a great editor and teacher.

This book is for my three favorite ladies—Eileen, Quinn and Kellyn. The Money Mammals simply wouldn't exist without you.

www.themoneymammals.com

ISBN 978-0-9826820-3-6

12 11 10 9 8 7 6 5 4 3 2 1

Printed in the U.S.A.

Joe the Monkey loved working at Vine. He loved the shop's owner, Mr. Gibbons, and he loved that they gave free vine-swinging safety lessons to every monkey who purchased a vine. With the county tournament coming up, business was booming.

"You can try the kaboom-kerbuzzler on this new vine," said Joe to the small simian he was helping. "Here, let me show you." Joe squatted on his furry haunches and sprung upward to catch the sturdy vine before going into an expert swing.

On the way home from Vine, Joe stopped to see his good friend, Piggs the Bank, to work on songs for his other love, The Money Mammals band. Piggs had just been to the store and could not contain his excitement.

"Have you seen my new green STUFF? Everybody is collecting it! Sweet swine, Joe! You need to get some. It's only $9.99!"

"You know that's ten dollars, right?...for...Stuff," said Joe. "What do you do with it anyway?"

"It's magical," whispered Piggs mysteriously, "Just look at it, Joe." Piggs was mesmerized as he pried open the top of the can like a prized jewel case. What Joe saw was hardly jewel-like. Sure, it glittered, but that was all. He snorted in disbelief and spoke more slowly, thinking Piggs hadn't heard him before.

"What...do...you...DO...with it?"

"Do with it?" Piggs piped, "You don't DO anything. It's Stuff!"

Piggs had more to tell.

"I used the money from my Spend Smart jar – all the money I've been making working at Mud, Mess & More. Smart thinking, huh, Joe?"

"Not exactly," said a skeptical Joe, "You used ALL your Spend Smart money on THAT?"

"But, Joe, it's magical," Piggs gushed. "Just look at it!"

"Must be magical," observed Joe, "because all your Spend Smart money just disappeared."

Joe and Piggs went to pick up Clara J. Camel for band practice.
Joe's sister, Marmoset, was already there.
"Clara," said Joe, as he waited, "Can you believe that Piggs is collecting that Stuff? What IS that Stuff anyway?"
"Uh, I'm not sure," Clara noted as she stole a glance at his sister.
"Marmoset, time to go," urged Joe. "Get your things together."

"Not things, Joe. STUFF!" cried Marmoset. "Only $9.99 each. And it's magical!"
"Not you too?" groaned Joe.

The next day Joe ran into Vargas the Vulture.
The normally grumpy bird chirped like a songbird.
"Looky, what I just got," he announced. "Yellow!"
"Blazin' Bananas," droned Joe, "Don't tell me. It's..."
"Magical!" beamed the interrupting bird as he continued. "You're into Stuff too?" the bird asked.
"I've heard about it," Joe murmured.

"Then you probably heard that the new Big Giant store has it ON SALE starting tomorrow!" announced Vargas. "Stuff for $4.99! Talk about magical!

And you better start looking for another job, my baboon buddy. Big Giant sells vines cheap too, much less than your expensive snappy swingers at Vine."

Later that night, a worried Joe talked to his mother. "Look, Mom, the vines Mr. Gibbons sells are cheaper at Big Giant. How can Mr. Gibbons keep Vine in business and make money?"

"I think he'll be ok," she said brightly. "He sells high-quality vines."

Joe wasn't so sure.

"Well, maybe Mr. Gibbons could bring his prices down," Joe's father suggested. Joe liked that idea. He decided to tell his boss the next morning.

Joe told Mr. Gibbons the bad news.
"We charge $20 for a SuperVine 3000. Big Giant has one like it for $10," he explained.
"But our vines are better quality," said Mr. Gibbons, "and don't forget that we offer a free lesson. Besides, I can't bring my prices down and stay in business. Ms. Swine over at Mud, Mess & More is in trouble, too. Big Giant is selling slop for half the price she does."
Joe knew Mr. Gibbons was right and hoped that the vine-swinging team would be smart about their spending and not get hurt.

The next day Joe walked with Clara to band practice.
"What is up with Piggs and Marmoset? Can't they see that Stuff is just... worthless? Now they're telling all their friends to shop at Big Giant for Stuff."
"They'll come around," Clara assured him.
"But, it might be too late for Vine and Mud, Mess & More when they do," said Joe.
"Maybe you should tell Piggs that," she suggested.
Good point, thought Joe. Piggs probably didn't know about Mud, Mess & More's troubles.

Joe decided to talk to Piggs before band practice.
"Piggs, my family is NOT going to shop at Big Giant," he proclaimed proudly, "because they might put Vine out of business."

"Are you losing your monkey mind, big brother?" blurted a surprised Marmoset. "Their Stuff is HALF price."
"Marmoset, it might be cheaper, but you really are wasting your money," said Joe.

"Wasting her money?" Piggs objected.
"Nonsense! More Stuff comes out tomorrow, and it's RAINBOW!"
"But, Piggs," said Joe, "Mud, Mess & More might go out of business too."

The pig suddenly turned pale.
"Then I won't be able to make money to buy more Stuff!" cried the panicked porker.
"What do we do, Joe?"

The next morning, Joe and Piggs went to Big Giant.

"This is embarrassing," cried Piggs, holding his sign as excited shoppers elbowed their way through the crowd to be first in the door.

"Get out of my way, boys!" yelled Vargas, flapping his long feathery wings through the crowd. "They have the new Rainbow Stuff here today...I WON'T be denied."

Marmoset, the first inside, raced past Joe on her way out to tell all her friends the news.

"They're giving away a free Thing with every Stuff we purchase!" she cried, admiring her new Stuff AND Thing.

"Wait a second!" exclaimed Joe. "How did you get in there without us seeing you?"

"You know what they say...the early monkey gets the Stuff," she replied.

Joe could not believe it. Even his little sister couldn't control herself. But it was about to get worse...

"And here's that Stuff YOU wanted, Piggs," Marmoset mouthed to the porker.

Piggs wildly grabbed for it.

"WHAT? You too?" yelped Joe. "You're supposed to be helping me save Vine and Mud, Mess & More."

"Joe, this Stuff is just too hard to pass up. It's RAINBOW!" he oinked. "A swine's gotta do what a swine's gotta do!"

Joe began to think that maybe they were right. Maybe it was he. Maybe this Stuff WAS great. How could everyone else be wrong? After all, $4.99 for Stuff – how could anyone pass up such a great deal? But one question still nagged at him. What do you do with all that Stuff?

Despite Joe's warning, everyone in Coconut Valley shopped at Big Giant. Joe and Mr. Gibbons saw far fewer customers. Then the worst thing happened.

"You've done an incredible job, Joe, but Vine isn't going to make it. No one is buying, and monkeys just don't seem to care about good vines anymore. County tournament time is usually our biggest selling season, but the little swingers are all going to Big Giant."

There had to be a way to save Vine, thought Joe, but how?

The next day at school, Joe's friend, Screecher, tried out the kaboom-kerbuzzler – a very difficult move – and went flying into a wall at vine-swinging practice.

"Screecher, are you ok?"
"That hurt," Screecher whimpered.
"Crummy Big Giant vine! It's already broken."
"I have an idea," said Joe, comforting his little friend. "Let's go to Vine. With the tournament coming up, we've got to get you a better vine."

After school, Joe and Screecher headed over to Vine.

"I'll tell you what, Joe, Big Giant doesn't do repairs," said Mr. Gibbons afterhe examined the shredded vine. "Let's just replace his vine. He can pay the difference."

"That's very nice of you," said Joe, "but Screecher's mom just lost her job at Mud, Mess & More because of Big Giant. You can take the money out of my last paycheck."

"Joe, you don't have to do that. Get little monkey man here a new vine... and give him a free lesson like we would with any customer."

Screecher beamed.

Later that day, Screecher's friend, Sammie, came to the store.

"My vine broke too," Sammie said. "Screecher said you might be able to help me out."

"You bet we can," said gentle Mr. Gibbons.

Just before closing, Joe went in to tell his boss some good news.
"Word is spreading that our vines and service are the best."
"Joe, you did a wonderful job telling others about the quality of our vines, and someday I know you'll be a better businessman than I, but I can't keep up. Big Giant is just too big. We're still losing money. We have to close the store."

Joe was having a tough time focusing at band practice after telling his friends about Vine, until...

"Let's hold a benefit concert!" exclaimed Clara.

"Now THAT'S good thinking," chimed Piggs.

"Mud Mess & More is really in trouble. Can we help them too?"

"Of course," said Joe, but he remained worried.

"That IS a great idea, Clara, but Vine is closing tomorrow."

That night Joe was still confused.
"How can Vine close when people are starting to figure out that Big Giant vines are no good?"
"That's a good question, son," Joe's mother said, "and we're not sure why, but we are so proud of you."
"You did everything you could to help Mr. Gibbons stay in business," said Joe's father. "You're a clever little monkey."
"Thanks. But I didn't do enough."

As he drifted to sleep that night, Joe still worried. He tossed and turned all night as he thought about what would happen to Mr. Gibbons if Vine closed. The next morning, though, an idea struck Joe like a hot, zinging, lightning bolt. "My money jars! I can bring ALL my jars to help Mr. Gibbons!"

That morning, on the way to Vine, Joe ran into a less-than-perky Piggs. "I guess you were right, Joe. My new Stuff is not very magical anymore. It's all cracked and dried. What can I DO with this... junk? I didn't spend smart. I feel like a pig in a slopless trough." Just then, something caught Joe's attention.

There was a HUGE line leading to Vine.

Joe ran to the store on swift monkey feet. Breathless, he flew through the front door.

"All these little swingers need their vines replaced before the tournament," chattered Mr. Gibbons as he tried to keep up with all the customers.

"Big Giant pulled all their vines off the shelves because they were falling apart too easily."

Joe grinned from ear to ear.

"Looks like we're back in business!" exclaimed Mr. Gibbons, "Thanks to you!"

Right outside the store, Joe and Piggs found a broken-hearted bird.

"Look at all this...Stuff!" cried Vargas. "It's worthless!"

"I guess buying things cheaper isn't always spending smart, huh?" asked Piggs.

"Yeah, and I guess there's a difference between selling vines cheap and selling cheap vines," said Joe.

The next weekend, Mud, Mess & More got some much-needed help from the Money Mammals. The county tournament's new champs arrived to entertain, swinging on their sturdy new vines. Returning to the slop quality they had once enjoyed and then missed, pig customers soon returned to Mud, Mess & More. The Big Giant saga had come to a close. Joe's friends learned how to Spend Smart and no one spoke of Stuff or Thing anymore. Joe was the happiest monkey in Coconut Valley. His advice had finally worked like magic.

Made in the USA
Monee, IL
05 November 2026

67379802R00021